This Message Is For You!

365 Micro Motivators

to encourage you to act.

By: Cynthia I. Wilson

First Edition

Cover Photograph by Cynthia I. Wilson.
Separator Design by Harmony Kulp.

Produced in the United States of America.

Author Provided Cataloging Data
Wilson, Cynthia I., 1976-
    This Message Is For You: 365 Micro Motivators to encourage you to act. / Cynthia I. Wilson.
    191 p.   23 cm.
ISBN 979-8-9858090-2-2 (pbk)
   1. Motivation 2. Spirit Messages I. Title.
BF 501 .W746 2025
158.1--dc21

"Action is the foundational key to all success." – Pablo Picasso

Introduction

Have you ever felt like there was something more for you, but you didn't know what to do? The Micro Motivators in this book will give you the simple nudge that you need to move forward with something new or to expand what has limited you. Life can get so busy that you can simply forget to do the little things. This book also serves as a reminder to do the little things that help your health and wellbeing. My hope is that you will find at least one thing in this book that causes you to take action that creates change in your life and makes it even better than it is today. Sometimes a small action can make a big difference in your life.

I began writing this book in November 2019. I had gotten into a practice of daily meditation typically listening to shamanic drumming and from that I received messages of the day from my spirit guide George and many others as I continued this practice throughout 2020. I then reflected on each of those messages which is what you see in the writings below each message. The additional writings certainly incorporate my experience as a mother, daughter, friend, wife, life coach, manager, and nature lover.

However, I did not feel that the message of the day was just for me. Their wisdom could not be mine alone and this is why I am compelled to share the messages with you. You can choose to read this book from cover to cover. Or you can flip through and pick your favorite number or one that keeps coming up in your life. The important thing to remember is that this message is for you.

Acknowledgments

To my friend, Valerie Fahie, thank you for the continual encouragement to pursue this endeavor. I am so grateful for your positive impact on my life. To my family, Chris, Harmony, and Shane, thank you for your love and giving some time for the meditation and reflection needed to put all this together.

To my siblings & work colleagues, thanks for always listening to my ideas and offering suggestions. Bev, Bob, & Josh, your feedback has been extremely helpful. To Kathryn Johnson, whose courses through the Writer's Center helped keep me on track. Thanks also to Rebecca Austill-Clausen for talking with me about the various publication options and providing direction on this book. To my spiritual guides and teachers whose guidance led this book into being. To Michelle Jackson for her guidance on editing through her workshop. And to those at the Philadelphia's Writer's Conference 2023 for their encouragement and support.

Thanks also to those who have listened to this idea along the way and provided encouragement or feedback.

1. Be at peace with your decision.

Rest assured that your actions are true to your path. Step away from chaos. Take some time to meditate. Trust that all will work out.

2. Use your smile to turn someone's day around.

You are a beautiful part of this world. You have a purpose to fulfill. There is value to you being here. Your unique skills and perspectives are needed here.

3. It's up to you to turn the tide.

If you don't like the direction things are going, then make a change. It is under your control to make the adjustments needed to get on the desired course. You have the oar and can make a shift.

4. Take the time to rest.

You are working too hard. Step away. Take a nap. If that is not possible then go to bed early tonight.

5.   Quiet your mind and listen.

You are too distracted. Escape from the noise around you. Find your inner voice. Take a yoga or meditation class. Be free from technology for at least twenty minutes.

6.   Enjoy the process.

There is no need to rush. Take your time. You will get to your destination right when you need to be there. It is better to arrive late and be safe.

7.   Amplify joy within yourself.

Stop looking to others to find happiness. You need to look within. Once you have found joy there, it will become easier to share with others. Begin your inner refection.

8.   Don't be afraid to say, "I love you."

Don't let fear hold you back from saying how you feel. You don't want to miss your opportunity to do so. Time and connections pass quickly. It is better to know now than ask yourself later, "what if?"

9. Enjoy the simple things.

Cook a meal from scratch. Watch a bird fly. Smell the flowers. Spend time with loved ones. Find satisfaction in the small things.

10. Check at least one thing off your to-do list.

It's time to get back into action. You do not need to conquer everything. Find a sense of accomplishment in just getting one thing done.

11.   Make the time to learn something new.

Watch a video. Take a class. Read a book. It's time to explore a new topic that motivates you. Focus on that topic for at least thirty days.

12.   Stay Grounded.

It's not the time to daydream of vacation or lofty ideas like winning the lottery. Keep your feet on the earth. Look at the responsibilities in front of you. And get them done.

13.   Take a "Me" day.

Go to your favorite place. Treat yourself. Do something just for you. It is important to connect with the things you love to do.

14.   Pay attention to your dreams.

Your subconscious mind is sending you messages. Listen to them. Analyze what they could mean. Tell a friend.

15.   Write down your ideas.

Put those thoughts to pen and paper. You have great ideas. Jot them down and then prioritize which one needs action first.

16.   Stick with it.

Your work will be meaningful to others. Don't give up. Keep progressing and you will look back and be glad you did. Be persistent.

17.　Explore the possibility of something new.

Change is inevitable. You can choose to embrace it or let it happen. How you control change or react to it has an impact on your happiness. Be open to new opportunities.

18.　Stop. Listen. And be present.

Remove distractions and pay attention. You need to observe what is happening around you. Be there for a friend in need. Put the phone down and be the source of comfort.

19.   Watch a new television series.

Step out of your reality for a little bit. Study the characters. Pick one and put yourself in their shoes. Would you have taken the same actions that they did?

20.   Find spots of smooth sailing when the water seems rough.

Look for areas of respite throughout your day. Recognize when it is time to escape. Take a step back from any challenge to give yourself clear context on the situation.

21.   Watch silly animal videos.

Enjoy your favorite comic. Tell some jokes and enjoy laughter with those around you. Have a good laugh. Let joy be a part of your day.

22.   Go out of your way to help someone today.

Hold the door open for someone. Buy a coffee for the person in the car behind you in line. Take a simple action to make a difference in another person's day.

23. Notice the beauty around you.

Look at the water droplets on leaves. Gaze at the sun or the moon. See the beauty in all who and that you encounter today.

24. Express Gratitude.

Show how grateful you are not just for the big things, but also for the little things. Recognize how blessed and lucky you are. Set the intention for what is to come. Give thanks for what you are to receive in the future as well.

25. Press the reset button.

If what you are doing is not working, explore a new approach. Take a few steps back and begin again. Review your intentions for what you are working towards and adjust your direction appropriately.

26. Reach out to a friend.

Pick up the phone and call a friend who you have been missing. Send an e-mail or a text message to reconnect. Just let them know that you are thinking about them. Find a way to get in touch with them.

27.   Describe the vision.

Define how you want things to unfold in your life. Where do you see yourself? What is it going to take to get there? Set your course of action. Concentrate on what makes you happiest. Write down the steps to get there.

28.   Let others comfort you.

We all deal with challenges in life. It is ok to recognize when you've had enough. Have a good cry. Ask for the help that you need. Accept assistance from those offering. You don't always have to be the strong one.

29.   Inventory your to-dos.

Make an action list. Decide what is most worthy of your attention in the coming days, weeks, or months. Use that list to guide your actions.

30.   Inspire others by your example.

Share the wonderful things that you are doing with others. You never know what impact you can have on others. Something so small can inspire action in others. Everyone can make a difference.

31.   Look at things from a different perspective.

Seek out or be open to another's point of view. Reconsider your position. Try exploring a new angle to view the situation in front of you. Change your mindset.

32.   Get out of bed.

Say goodbye to darkness. Let the light come in. Rid your life of the things that don't bring you happiness. Make the decision to be happy and share that happiness with others. You can choose how you feel.

33.   Share a special memory with a friend.

Remember something from your childhood that brought you joy. These are often pieces that molded us which another may never know. Share what brings you happiness.

34.   Have confidence in yourself.

You are on the right track. Each action, no matter how small, can have an impact. Keep going. You're doing what you need to do in this moment.

35.   Observe animal behavior.

Pay attention to the birds. Watch the animals that are around you. See what you can learn from their way of life and apply it to your own.

36.   Sit down for a family meal.

Sometimes life gets so busy that you can miss the simple joys of connecting. Reach out to others and gather around a table. Food can bring people together.

37.   Plant the seed.

If you want to get your idea out there and watch it grow, you must first plant the seed. Plants can't grow without water and sunshine. Your idea can't grow if it is never exposed to the elements. Put yourself out there.

38.   Practice positive self-talk.

You are amazing. Now practice saying, "I am amazing!" Recognize how it makes you feel. Capture any negative thoughts and then let them go. Adjust how you talk to yourself to be more positive when you are feeling down.

39.   Find a way to remove what is blocking you from your goal.

Often what is blocking us is our own barrier. It is not fruitful to blame another. Examine the actions that you have taken to pursue your goal and what else you can do.

40.   Watch the sunrise or sunset.

Sunrises can help us with new beginnings. Sunsets can provide closure or endings. Enjoy the beauty of nature as it relates to your current situation. Begin anew or let go.

41.   Play the drum.

Pick up a musical instrument. Experiment with making new sounds. Let the sound resonate through your body.

42.   Share a memory of a friend who passed away.

Allow your memories of a friend to live on by sharing a story of how they impacted your life. Talk to another person about a fun moment that you shared. If a song brings about a memory of one who has passed, share it with others.

43. Look within yourself for true happiness.

Material items and other people are not going to make you happy. The next shiny object is only temporary happiness. Understand what makes you smile without an object or a person. Focus on you.

44. Consider the opportunities in front of you.

You have potential for growth. It is ok to explore the possibilities before committing to change. You have until the contract is signed to make your decision.

45. Speak with intention.

Be purposeful in what you say to others. Understand your audience. Concentrate on the outcome that you wish to receive. Be direct and kind.

46. Tune out the noise.

Unsubscribe to shop e-mails. Hide the ads. Unplug from your devices for a little while. Shift your attention to what is important.

47.   Accept with loving kindness.

Understand the meaning and effort behind anything that you receive. Recognize that perception and judgement are a sense of entitlement. The gesture is more valuable than the object.

48.   Stay focused on the task at hand.

Direct your attention to what needs to be completed. Don't let interruptions take you away from what you need to achieve. Keep going the course. You will feel relieved when it is done.

49.   Connect with friends.

Reach out to those you have been missing. You don't have to go through this life alone. Friendship is a two-way street. Practice active listening.

50.   Examine why you are carrying the baggage.

Clutter has taken over in your mind or body. It's time to forgive yourself or another and wipe the slate clean. Brush off that weight from your shoulders.

51.   Explore uncharted territory.

Travel to a unique destination. Dive into something exciting. Break free from the routine and find a new favorite place.

52.   Brainstorm your future.

Look towards the future and think about where you want to be. Act on the tasks you need to complete to get there. If you can see something that is likely to become a problem, then fix it before it gets there. Planning is powerful.

53.   Register for a workshop.

Learn a new skill. Connect with others who share your enthusiasm on a topic. Go ahead and register for that class you have been contemplating.

54.   Take notes.

Inspiration can go as easily as it has come through. It is important to accurately capture the details. Write it down so you do not forget a key piece of information. You may need to reflect on it in the future.

55.   Tell someone.

You are holding on to information and it is bubbling up inside. You need to share it with another person. There is no need to hold burdens or successes inside. Tell a trusted source.

56.   Plan a trip.

Now that you have spent time daydreaming about going somewhere special, it is time to finally get the reservations in place. Look to your calendar for any potential conflicts. Double check your dates and locations before clicking purchase. Then get ready to pack your bags and go.

57. Schedule time with a family member.

Make the effort to reach out to a family member who you have not seen in a while. Grab a drink to catch up. Enjoy some time reminiscing and discussing the future.

58. Understand that others may be going through a hard time.

Remember that what you don't like in someone else is often what you don't like about yourself. We are all connected. Approach everyone with love so it will grow.

59.   Serve from the heart.

When you think about sharing items with others connect to what the other person may need or want. Find correlations between your loves and theirs to connect deeply and give with meaning.
Show that you care.

60.   Thank a teacher.

Look back at those who have made an impact on your life and share appreciation for their influence. We can be taught valuable lessons by people of all ages. If the most impactful person is no longer around, then share their story with another person.

61.   Find your motivation.

Think about those things that make you feel alive. Look for ways to garner that feeling today. Seek inspiration and act. Let yourself be free.

62.   Navigate through the winds of change.

Sometimes we wish the course was charted for us exactly with no surprises. This time there is no map and no plan. Allow yourself to express curiosity to see where this goes. Stop thinking about how prescribed it should be for you.

63. Dig for information.

It is time to go deeper into the research for information that you are seeking. Go to your local library for help. If this information is more of a personal nature, try a counselor or hypnotist.

64. Find quiet among the chaos.

Step away for a moment. Know when you have had enough. Joining the activity might just not be your thing. Recognize when it is causing more stress than you can handle.

65.   Ride the wave.

Things are changing around you. It is alright. Ride it out and see where it takes you. There can be calmness on the shore or great adventures in the ocean. This is part of your plan.

66.   Take care of something that you have been neglecting.

Explore your barrier to completing a certain task. Why do you keep putting it off? It is time to move past it and get it done. You will feel so much better that you did.

67.   Tell a silly joke.

Give those around you a chuckle by sharing your sense of humor. Lighten the mood with a little silliness. Share a tear-inducing laugh with a friend.

68.   Observe your world.

Pay attention to what is going on around you. Seek to investigate the world beneath your feet. Watch current events to be aware of what is going on in the world.

69.   Take a step back.

You are in too deep. Your viewpoint is on the details. You need to observe the bigger picture of what is going on. Seek a change in position to see the situation from a different angle.

70.   Drink more water.

Hydration is important for your body to function well. Make sure that you are getting enough water. Remember to drink a little extra after a massage, workout, or healing session.

71.   Share that photo.

Go ahead and bring up a fun memory to share with others. It will bring a smile to their face. It is ok to show your nostalgia or creativity.

72.   Let your guard down and have fun.

Let loose a little. It is ok to break out of your shell. Dance through the day. Enjoy each moment.

73.   Thrive in your personal power.

Embrace your excellence. Stand tall in what you believe in. Stay true to yourself. Find your strength.

74.   Be the source of light.

When people are looking for good in the world, let them think of you. Be the shoulder for someone to cry on. Listen actively. Be the one who makes others smile, even, if only, for today.

75. Unlock the door of opportunity.

You have the key. Allow yourself to open the door to see what may be available. You can still decide if you want to enter, but if you never peek inside you will not know what opportunities are available to you.

76. Express Care and Compassion.

Allow yourself to care for another person. Have compassion for what they are going through. Try to understand the world from their point of view. Not all pain is visible.

77.   Compromise. Push back a little and give in a little.

Compromise allows for a give and take. Make sure that your dealings involve equality. Share the burden of the tasks ahead and they will feel lighter for all involved.

78.   Prepare yourself for what is next.

Start looking ahead for what is to come. Look at your calendar a few days ahead and make sure that you have everything that you need. Check your refrigerator to make sure you are not going to run out of anything important.

79. Persist. This is only the beginning.

This is the time for continual checks. You need to make sure that others are keeping up with their part of the bargain. Keep asking for what you want and need. Insist on it.

80. Develop your skills every day.

Gaining expertise takes time. Just a few minutes every day can make a difference. If you want to excel at something it requires that you practice.

81.   Look both ways.

Inspect all angles of a situation before moving on. A surprise could creep up on you unexpectedly if you are not paying attention. Once you have analyzed your surroundings then you can confidently move ahead.

82.   Play a game.

Pretend like you are a child. Allow the carefree joy to come into your day. Enjoy a game and the company of those who are with you.

83.   Spread kindness.

Do something nice for another person. Share a compliment to brighten someone's day. Let kindness be contagious.

84.   Know your equipment.

Open your mind and your heart, then your mouth. There are so many tools at your disposal. Peek inside to see how you can help yourself and others. Get to know your resources.

85.   Share your story.

Your experiences matter. Connections are built by sharing what is happening in your life. Knowing that someone is going through the same thing as you can release a burden.

86.   Soar to new heights.

Keep going. There is so much potential for you to achieve your dreams. Propel forward in the direction of your choice with confidence.

87.   Acknowledge a small victory.

Celebrate the win, no matter how small. Each step forward gets you closer to what you want to achieve. It's the pause to recognize a milestone that helps get you to the next step on the journey.

88.   Treasure the written word.

Look through old cards or letters.
Recognize the importance of writing things down. Open old journals or simply read a book.

89.   Get some fresh air.

Take a trip to the park or the beach. Enjoy the sunshine or the calm before the storm. Step out in the rain and be cleansed.

90.   Move the cares of the world away.

Get a massage. It is time for you to meditate. Be at peace with yourself. Look for ways to unwind.

91.   Help an elderly person.

Check on an elderly neighbor who may need assistance. Offer to run an errand or take groceries to the car for someone. Recognize the difference that you can make to provide ease in just a few minutes.

92.   Draw a picture.

Pull out a pen and paper and start to draw. Let whatever comes to mind flow through your hand. There is no pressure to create a masterpiece, just release the tension of the day through artwork.

93.   Cleanse your soul.

Evaluate what is going on inside. Speak your truth and be free of burdens. Forgive those whose transgressions you are holding on to. Be free.

94.   Make some popcorn and watch a movie.

Embark on another's journey for a short while. Live vicariously through what you see on the screen. Enjoy a treat and then contemplate the impact of what you have seen on your life.

95. Go out into the world.

Hiding in the corner will not help you to achieve your plans in life. You need to go out into the world. Let others celebrate you.

96. Throw your negative thoughts into a pit and walk away.

Rid yourself of the negative thoughts that pervade your mind. They no longer serve you. Surround yourself with those people who build you up. Brush the negativity off your body.

97.   Let your heart take you to success.

You know what you need to do so do it already. There is no need to question anymore. The path was laid out before you.

98.   Breathe new life into a project.

Pick up an unfinished project and rethink your approach. The world is still waiting for it. Remove the dust and move forward.

99.   Take the time to heal.

Recognize that your body needs time to heal. High activity levels are not contributing to your overall health. Give yourself recovery time. A little break can get your further next time.

100.   Blanket yourself in knowledge.

Dive deeper into subjects that interest you. Get cozy and read. Recognize that you can learn from all that is around you and all who are around you.

101.   Workout.

Lift some weights. Go for a run. Dance in your living room. Do some yoga. Your body needs movement.

102.   Remember something good about an acquaintance.

Let your memories help you reflect on important moments of your development and those along the way who helped, whether intentionally or unintentionally. Give them thanks for that part in your life. Smile at the fun times you have had.

103.　Move slowly and with intention.

Be like a gentle wind. Pass through your day calmly and swiftly. Exude peace. Help give someone else a little lift.

104.　Learn from the past.

Look at the patterns in your life which you have not been able to break. Examine your emotions and the outcomes. Keep those things that bring you joy and happiness. Work on changing the rest.

105.   See love in your future and it will be there.

To see love you need to be love. Envision yourself as the giver and let that help you to become the receiver. Write down what you'd like to have as a part of your life.

106.   Embrace patience.

Speeding through this will only cause mistakes. Don't rush. It's important to take your time. Be methodical through this process for the best possible outcome.

107. Relish your time in the spotlight.

Now is the time. It is your time to shine. Be proud of what you have accomplished and thank those who have helped you along the way. Enjoy a moment to pause and reflect before moving on to the next project.

108. Capture the moment.

Take a picture. Write about the impact this moment has for you. You will want to reflect on this in the future. Be present.

109. Zigzag through the needs of the day.

Sometimes it is necessary to jump from one thing to the next. While it may seem like you are doing so many things, take the appropriate amount of time on each thing that you need to do. You can still feel very accomplished with achieving small goals.

110. Design something new.

Pick up the canvas and create. Organize your space in a new way. Weave fabric together. Get out the pencil and paper and draw.

111.   Do the things that make you happiest.

Reflect on the skills that you have and use them today. Are you great at giving hugs or listening? Feel good about your contribution to your part of the world.

112.   Wipe the Counter.

It's time to clear some space. Get rid of any residual dirt. Start on a fresh surface.

113.   Get to work.

You just need to sit down and get things done. The project needs your attention. Waiting could cause an unwanted delay.

114.   Purify your soul.

Get rid of negative energy. Burn some sage or palo santo. Take a bath in Epson salt. Swim in a nearby body of water. Cleanse yourself.

115. Appreciate what is around you.

Put your phone down and look around. Take in the beauty that is in front of you. Go for a drive to a new place and enjoy the beauty that it has to offer. Don't miss the view.

116. Move like no one is watching.

Put on some music and dance. Allow yourself to remove some of the stress from your day. Expand your creativity in movement.

117.   Practice acceptance.

Sharing peace starts with one interaction. Connect with your neighbors who may be different from you. Learn something new about their culture. The more you learn, the more you understand, the more you can share with others.

118.   Revisit your childhood.

Look back at your upbringing. Reflect on the memories that come up to see what resonates. Recognize how they have brought you to where you are today. Consider the impact that it had on your life and world view.

119. Connect with what you love.

Concentrate on the things that bring you joy. Dedicate some time on those activities within your current abilities. If you have limitations where you can no longer do some of the things that you previously loved to do, then remember that feeling when you could.

120. Cultivate your skills.

If you want to get better at something, then you must develop it. Dedicate just a few minutes each day. Even prodigies need to practice their art.

121.　Look inside.

Stop ignoring the signals that your body is sending you. You need to take a further look at what is going on either physically or emotionally. It might be time to schedule that X-ray or ultrasound. Remember that it is ok to talk to someone for help.

122.　Go and explore.

Take an adventure. You just need a change of scenery. This can be as simple as a trip to the mall, a walk in the park, or as robust as a safari or a cruise. It is important to get out of the house.

123. Clean an area of your home.

Sometimes cleaning can be overwhelming. Just pick one spot to work on today. Maybe it is a junk drawer that should be dumped and gone through, or the fridge that has some old take out, or perhaps it is the junk mail that has piled up. Start small then repeat with another area until you feel satisfied.

124. Be Vigilant.

Be decisive and determined. Get things done. It is not the time to waver. Go forth with the courage that you've got this.

125. Know that what you are going through has purpose.

You are caught up in the emotion of what is going on around you and it can be difficult to think that it will stop. It is going to be ok. While it may be tough now, it is going to work out how it needs to in the end.

126. Embrace the nothing.

Be still. It is necessary to stop occasionally. Sit in silence. Rest. The chaos is bound to come back. Enjoy the pause.

127. Incorporate play into your day.

You need to bring a bit of joy into your day. Enjoy the laughter of others and join them. Even if you are on a video call, it is ok for others to hear you laugh. It is up to you to determine how you want to experience your day.

128. Change your perspective.

Lay on the floor. Climb to the top of a mountain. Sit in a different seat in the room. Give yourself a new view on the world around you. Open yourself up to new ideas.

129.   Bake, Make, Create.

It is time to put your ideas into production. Use your creativity to make something new. Try a new recipe and if you don't love it the first time, try it again with adjustments. There is a creative process that you need in your life. Learn from your mistakes and adjust.

130.   Seek the helpers.

There is a larger purpose to what you are going through. It is possible that your soul picked this path for you or others to learn and grow. You will survive this. Hope is a powerful gift.

131.   Hug yourself.

Celebrate your successes. Recognize when you have done something meaningful or accomplished your dream. It is important for you to love yourself and to acknowledge that you are making progress on your journey.

132.   Build a vision board.

Allow yourself to have some moments of reflection. Think about the things that you have accomplished and what you still want to do. This is a time for contemplation.

133. Eat some protein.

Your energy could use a charge. Seek items that will build your immune function. Increasing your protein intake today can help get your body what it needs.

134. Use your power to make a difference.

You have an impact on the world around you. Send the Earth healing and love. Your influence can produce a change. It can simply be recycling or reusing something in a new way. Find the connection with your environment.

135.   Spend time with your given or chosen family.

Treasure the people who surround and support you. Not all family is blood or marriage related, and they don't need to be. Savor both the tough times and the joy-filled ones.

136.   Set an intention.

What do you want to give the world today? What do you want to receive? Set forth your desires at the beginning of each day.

137.   Be flexible.

It is great to have plans, but often they need to change. You need to go with the flow. When the plan needs to be adjusted, it will be up to you to waver for the best outcome.

138.   Do some research.

Look at a map and explore where you want to go. Go to the library or bookstore to gather more details on the information that you need to be successful. Watch a program that will offer you the details you are missing. Seek more information on your interests.

139.   Be Grateful.

Gratitude is the greatest gift that you can give yourself. Taking time to recognize the good in each day helps you to see just how much good there is in the world. From there you can share that with others, which helps continue gratitude.

140.   Remember that hard times do not last forever.

This will all be a memory soon. Sometimes it is difficult to remember that when you are in the thick of a challenging period. Find the bright moments and remember that, while it may feel like the tough parts will never end, this is only temporary.

141.   Give 100%.

Be honest with yourself. Have you dedicated the time needed to achieve the outcome that you desire? Is your work structured and organized so that you are most efficient with your time and others? Put your best effort forward.

142.   Go outside.

Fresh air is exactly what you need. Just take a minute to feel the warm or cold air on your skin. Consider how other animals acclimate to the changing environment. Look around. You never know what you might see.

143.   Find Balance.

The scales are tipped, and your focus is leaning in one direction. Incorporate more balance in what you do, in how you eat, and how you care for your body. Equate work and family or friends on a more even level.

144.   Pursue your passion.

Gathering education is a wonderful thing. You must now put it into practice. You will truly excel the more that you invest in doing the work. Spend time with your passion project.

145.   Straighten your posture.

Roll your shoulders. Remove your slouch. Make sure that you are not leaning too much to one side or another. Wiggle your toes for balance. Understand your stance.

146.   Search for signs of hope.

Look for the good in the world. Find those things that make you feel like everything will be ok, like a smile, a song, a cardinal, a ladybug, a rainbow, or a four-leaf clover. See that the world is telling you that everything is going to be OK.

147.   Get in the game.

You have been standing on the sidelines too long waiting for your turn. It is time for you to play. Understand the importance of not only the competition itself, but also of being a part of the team.

148.   Create something new.

Use your creativity to express your feelings. Build upon old masters and share your unique talent. Be inventive with the materials that you have around you to form a new solution to an outstanding problem or issue. Your skills matter.

149.   Connect to the Earth.

Place your feet on the ground and feel the energy of the Earth. Look to the landscape before you. Feel the grass, the rocks, the sand, or the water beneath your feet. See the sky above you and all around you. Experience the senses of the elements and connect.

150.   Keep at it.

This is not the time to throw your hands in the air and give up. You need to persevere. Keep moving forward. If you need a change, then make it or ask for it as needed.

151.   Take a break.

You have worked so hard and now it is time to take a break. Relax before you take on the next project. Reflect on what went well and that which you would improve upon for next time. Enjoy a day of rest.

152.   Establish Reciprocity.

Give your loving vibes freely to others. This is about emotion not the physical self. Use acknowledgement and respect as a form of love. Be gracious with all that you receive back.

153.   Do something fun.

Play a video game. Paint a picture.
Journey through nature. Connect with a
friend and explore. Have an adventure.

154.   Revamp your style.

Be free to express yourself. Uniqueness is
valuable. Fear is only holding you back. Let
go of this fear. You can be anything that
you want.

155. Do what you can to help the world.

A grandiose plan is not needed to help the world. Plant a tree or flowers. Help someone who needs it. A small gesture or action can have a big impact.

156. Hold on.

You can make it through this. Life has many lessons for you. Sometimes in life the best way to recognize what you need to do is to show someone else. Find someone in a similar situation. Now write the advice that you would give them to get to the finish line. Follow your own advice.

157.   Write.

Pull out a journal and take some time to reflect on how far you have come. Get out the emotions that have been pent up. Release what you have been holding inside.

158.   Join the resistance.

Sometimes you need to simply give in and other times you need to fight for what is right. This is the time to fight. Join with others who share your cause and your passion.

159. Share laughter and love.

Be the sense of joy. Others are counting on you to bring them out of darkness. You are a light in this world.

160. See the writing on the wall.

The message you seek is right in front of you. Open your eyes to see it. Brush away the cobwebs for clarity.

161.   Chase rainbows.

Bring back your childlike joy and wonder. Set your worries aside and find something beautiful where you are now. Look at your environment with a renewed sense of curiosity.

162.   Even though the waters may change you, stay strong.

Ripples come into our lives to teach us. Learn to ride the wave. Eventually it will return you to the shore.

163. Trim the trees.

Clear your property. Remove any dead branches. Contact an arborist. Prepare yourself for any upcoming storms. Secure your property.

164. Talk to your neighbors.

Walk around your neighborhood and talk to others who are outside. You may find an unexpected connection. Enjoy the time with those around you.

165. Open the book.

Dive into another's world if only for a little while. Learn something new. Dedicate time to reading.

166. Track your credit cards.

It's time to review your finances. Confirm that everything is aligned and in order. If anything is out of sorts, then make a call to get it resolved.

167.   Enjoy your part in another's growth.

Use your talents to teach someone else what you know. Watch them develop their skills. See how they take the basics and move to the next level.

168.   When someone offers you help, accept it.

Assume good intentions. Everyone is not out to get you. This does not mean you are incapable. You just need assistance.

169.   Put your foot on the break.

If you continue to move fast, you will make mistakes and forget important tasks. Take a step back to analyze all that needs to be done. Slow down.

170.   Eat more fruits and vegetables.

In times of stress it is easy to ignore your nourishment. Look for the healthy options. Your body will thank you.

171.   Perform an act of kindness.

Tell a joke or give a compliment. Help turn another's day around. Do something to make someone else happy.

172.   Reformulate your question to get a clear answer.

There is so much that you want to learn. It can take some careful research. You may find the answers, but first you need to ask the right question.

173. Concentrate on some music.

Let the songs of others help your mind drift. Move to the beat. Bring out your own instrument. Let it take that stress away.

174. Seek out the little ones.

Watch a child. Look at their creativity, their curiosity, and their observations. Emulate their approach.

175. Watch some sports.

Observe how the teams work together. Think about how the rules of the game provide structure. See how the individual contributors are recognized by those around them. Feel the excitement of the crowd.

176. Review the past to change course.

Learn your lesson from what has happened before. The answer does not rest with what is yet to come. It has already been done. Seek a new approach this time.

177.   Let others deal with their own mess.

You must stop cleaning up after everyone else. They need to learn to do it on their own. You can provide instruction, but they need to do the work.

178.   Share your viewpoint.

Let another know one thing that you have encountered in life. It will give them an understanding of your story. Don't hold back.

179.   Simplify your belongings.

Clear out what is no longer meaningful.
Donate items that can still be used.
Organize what you want to keep and get
rid of what no longer serves you well.

180.   Read the signs.

The answer is right in front of you. Listen to
the message received and act. The signs
will tell you where to go.

181.   Clean the sink.

Wash any dishes. Wipe away any hard water stains. Clear the drain or run the garbage disposal. Remove any debris from the edges.

182.   Do your homework.

Stay current with the tasks that you need to accomplish. You can achieve your dreams. You just need to get through some of the basics first.

183. Reflect on your life choices.

Seize a memory and allow it to take you on a journey to the past. This reflection will show you how far you have come in life. Take stock in your accomplishments.

184. Charge your device.

It is time for a recharge. Get the extra rest you need. When you awaken make sure that you have the tools you need readily available.

185. Smile with nature.

See the trees sway. Peer into a pond and the surrounding landscape. Look at the crescent moon. Find whatever brings you joy outside.

186. Be aware of your empathy.

You are carrying the weight of the world. It is time to release it. Put your back against a surface and let it roll off.

187.   Catch the fish.

Go after what you want. Be open to the
chance that is coming towards you.
Reach out and grab the opportunity.
Don't let it slip out of your hands.

188.   Bounce Around.

You need a little bit of exercise. Jump on
the trampoline if you are able. Try a little
cross-fit or high intensity interval training.
Move quickly from one thing to the next.

189.　　Trust your instincts.

You know what is best in the situation. Why do you second guess yourself? Listen to that inner voice. Trust that you know what is best.

190.　　Read an article on a topic of interest to you.

Expand your knowledge of a new topic. Greater depth brings greater rewards. Take a new perspective or decide to jump into something new.

191.   Bring joy and hope to others.

You have a special place in this world. Be the light in the dark times. You are a star in the night sky. Shine Brightly.

192.   Give a loved one a hug.

Reach out and make the connection to a loved one. Connect your energy in an embrace. Show your love.

193.   Calmly express your emotions.

It is easy to rush to anger. It is harder to assess why you may feel it. Take a moment to reflect. Then move forward with discussing that which stirs your emotion.

194.   Listen to what is in your heart.

Sounds can come from many directions like a creaky chair, a crumbled paper, or a bird chirping. They can also come from within as a feeling. Tap into that and ask for what is needed for your best self.

195.   Sit in the path of illumination.

Get some vitamin D from the sun. Turn on the light. Recognize the path is there for you and connect with it.

196.   Water the plants.

This is a reminder for you to take care of the things that need it. Maybe you do just need to water the plants or maybe you need to take care of yourself or a loved one? Give attention to the things or people that need it.

197. Decorate or redecorate a room.

Sometimes you need to move things around to make the most out of your space. Give it a purpose. If it no longer has a use, then it's time to make a change.

198. Drink some tea.

Switch from soda or coffee for one drink. Explore different flavors to find one that you like. See if adding creamer or honey makes a difference for you. Try European traditions or Japanese Tea Ceremonies.

199. Discipline yourself.

It's up to you to achieve what you want in your day. Invest the time to lay it out and find the balance between work and play. Keep yourself to that schedule.

200. Recognize that every small part is still important.

When you look at things from above, we are all just small fish. We are a microcosm of a much larger picture in this universe. Look at an insect, like the bee, and realize your own value in this world.

201.　Catch the frog and shed your skin.

Make sure that you are ready for the changes to come. Utilize the rich nutrients of the earth to sustain you. Rid yourself of that barrier that is holding you back.

202.　Take respite in the shadow.

You have been in the spotlight for so long. It is time to lay low. Let others shine. Use the time to recharge.

203.   Take the call.

Answer the phone as it can bring about new opportunities. If you feel compelled to do something new, then trust that it is the right time. Be open to the possibilities.

204.   Be a conduit.

It is your turn to be the messenger. Let the information flow through you. Don't be afraid to share it.

205.   Go to the woods.

Spend time with the trees. Breathe in the fresh air. Enjoy nature's wonder. Try forest bathing.

206.   Choose your words and actions as if you are talking to yourself.

There is a connection between us all. A greater force that unites us to be here in this time and this place. Connect to each other with this in mind. We are all one.

207.   Get rid of interference.

It is easy to be distracted. Finish what you start. Make plans for what else needs to be accomplished.

208.   Take out the trash.

Don't leave the garbage piled in the corner. Move it to a place of proper disposal. It is holding you back.

209. Center yourself.

Things may have gotten a little out of hand. Shift your focus. Find the balance that you crave.

210. Maintain your progress.

You may feel as if you want to give up on that project, but you should continue. The rewards on the other side of this are worth it. Don't give up now.

211.   Glance at the sky and dream of possibilities.

The world is not as shut off as you think. Dream of what you want your future to be. Think big.

212.   Make the call.

You may have a difficult decision in front of you. Prolonging the outcome will not change the inevitable. It's time to decide how to proceed and move forward.

213.   Challenge yourself.

Walk or run in a 5K race. Go kayaking. Jump rope. Do a cartwheel. Push the boundaries of what you have done so far in your life.

214.   Change the law.

The most impactful thing that you can do is to work on the governing laws. If you don't like something, then strive to change it. Work for the benefit of all people.

215.   Dive deeper into learning.

Study the topics that interest you. Recognize that you are only skimming the surface. There is still more for you to learn. Invest in the opportunities that present themselves.

216.   Forge your own path.

You don't need to follow the crowd. Make your own way in this world. Share your exclusive outlook on life.

217.   See the light at the end of the tunnel.

The long road that you have been on is about to see daylight. Reflect on where you have been. Recognize that the best is yet to come.

218.   Paint the picture.

Share your vision with your community. Describe the scenery. Be creative. Color your world.

219.   Go camping.

Tell stories around a fire. Have some smores. Play flashlight tag or cards. Sing with friends or family. Have some time away from technology.

220.   Manage the distractions.

Turn notifications off to keep you on the task at hand. Keep your eyes on the prize. You will hit the bull's eye if you can concentrate.

221.　Follow the right path.

Find it within you to go that extra mile for someone. Treat others with kindness. Work for the greatest good.

222.　Know when to hold tight.

Let strategy help you get to the end that you seek. Remain patient. The immediacy that you desire may not be to your best advantage. Pause.

223. Know when to let go.

There are some games that you will not win and that is alright. The best creative solutions can come from a perceived failure. Let it fuel you to go in a different direction.

224. Work towards completion.

There may be a long path to your destination. Keep the effort up to reach your mark. See any set-back as an opportunity for growth. Take one step forward.

225.   Make a deal.

Barter your talents and skills. Make the trade. Find the art of negotiations and explore it. It's time to complete that paperwork.

226.   Stop procrastinating now.

Don't let fear stop you from achieving your dreams. It's time to go after what you want. What are you waiting for?

227.   Color a picture.

Give your drawing some flare. Add some shading or gradients. Show that there is more than black and white in your life.

228.   Give up your spot in line.

Let another person have the last item. Get help for someone in need. Do something simple to make someone else's day special.

229.   Wish them well.

Forgive those who hurt you. Don't let them continue to have a hold on you. Cut the cord. Send them peace and you will receive it yourself.

230.   Trust the process.

You've got this. You have prepared for this moment and can move forward confidently. It is alright if it seems a bit slow. There is always room to improve.

231.   Turn down the volume.

Quiet the mind. Take things slowly. Listen to the other things going on around you.

232.   Look into your ancestry.

Discover your roots. How far back can you track your ancestors? Learn more about the towns in which your relatives lived or find the local history organization for your town or county.

233.   Stay true to yourself.

Stick to your own convictions. Understand what you need and don't change who you are or what you believe just to feel accepted. Follow your own way.

234.   Learn to love yourself.

If you are feeling alone in the world, know that loved ones are always by your side. Radiate that love back to others. Then you will find the happiness that you seek.

235.   Nourish the soil.

Compost your scraps and let life grow. Turn it periodically. The world is yours. Take care of it like a child.

236.   Buy the recliner.

Make sure that you have a comfortable place to relax in your home. You have been working hard and could use a little reprieve. Allow yourself the time to decompress, read a book, or watch some tv.

237.   Carve out time for your own interests.

Make sure you are finding ways to fulfill your heart's desire. Create! Dance! Write!

238.   Recognize your building blocks.

Reflect on the thoughts, actions, and influences that brought you to where you are today. Understanding your journey is just as important, if not more so, then knowing where you are now. Seek to break down your barriers. Be grateful for your path.

239. Circle in on what you want.

It's time to move in closer to get what you want in life. Narrow in on your desire. Go for it!

240. Enjoy playing the game.

It is not about whether you win or lose. It is spending time with friends that matters. There are also lessons that you learn in the process to become a better player. Approach the game with that mindset.

241.   Brush off negativity.

It is not about you. Do not take this personally. Let it go. Continue to do what you need to do.

242.   Break it down.

You have a big task ahead of you. Try not to get overwhelmed. Split the work into manageable parts and you will feel in control.

243. Use your voice.

Do not hide in the shadows. Be confident in your knowledge and ability. Speak up.

244. Get it done.

You have the allotted time and the tools, but you need to use the time wisely. Stay centered and take appropriate breaks to refresh, but don't lose sight of your objective.

245.   Analyze disappointment.

It is ok if not everything goes your way. Think about what you could have done differently. It is important to express your feelings but then also to let them go. It just means something better is around the corner.

246.   Learn a new recipe.

Ask friends for a new recipe. Or share one that you recently made with others. Food can bring people together even when they are far apart.

247.   Listen to the rocks.

The earth holds our history. Pause and listen to her story. Look to your own life to determine what builds you up and what breaks you down.

248.   Follow your dream.

You must keep going for what you believe in. When something truly resonates with you that is when you know it is worth it. Your hard work will pay off. It's not just about the final product, review the journey that got you here.

249.   Incorporate exercise into your day.

Take a walk. Ride your bike. Spend a few minutes on the treadmill. Or simply do some stretches. It's time to put your body in motion.

250.   Feel the cool breeze.

You have been running too hot. Take a moment to cool down. Breathe deeply and feel the wind. If there is no breeze, grab some ice or take a cold shower.

251.   Stand tall like a tree.

Hold on to solid ground. Weather any storms that come your way. Move your arms to reach the sun. Get in touch with your roots.

252.   Perceive the beauty in diversity.

Include those who may have a different perspective in your conversation. It is important to see all sides and understand the why behind it. Everyone has an important contribution.

253. Check your own reflection.

Make sure that you are putting out into the world what you would like to see. The view in the mirror should show you the qualities that you love. Focus on your strengths.

254. Study the clouds for inspiration.

The sky is constantly changing just like us. When you view the movement, you can begin to recognize your own. Use your creativity.

255.   Monitor your language.

Communication needs to be clear to get your point across. At the same time, you need to understand how the other person may react to your message. Edit until there is no room for misunderstanding. Be sure to listen along the way.

256.   Support the arts.

Go to a gallery, a concert, or a theater production. Ensure that your local community is protecting the arts. Become inspired by the work of others.

257.   Be mindful of your volume.

Getting excited about something is great. Acknowledge if you want the world to know if you are happy or angry about something. Your tone can create lasting impressions.

258.   Convert those points and get your reward.

Review financial strategies that can benefit you. Implement changes for long term help. Make your money work for you.

259.   Invest in your home.

Your home should be a comforting place. The more peace you feel there the more that you can bring into the world. Make the changes necessary to make your space your own.

260.   Love one another.

Remember that the more love you give the more you receive. Love is stronger than hate and causes less stress. Envision a world full of peace.

261. Take care of yourself.

Know the importance of self-care. Speak up when you need some time for yourself. When you take care of yourself you can provide better care for others.

262. Calculate the patterns.

Our behavior repeats. Try to identify the why behind habits that you want out of your life. It is time to focus on the patterns that bring you joy and to stop focusing on those which bring you pain.

263.   Go to the lake.

It is time to step away and go to a slower pace. Sit by a lake or a nearby water source and just watch. If you are comfortable dive in and let the water refresh you.

264.   Realize magical moments.

There are times in our lives where everything seems to align, recall them. Think about what you were doing in those times. Understand the impact that they had on your life. Seek them now.

265. Share your idea.

Speak up about that which is meaningful to you. Ask questions to get the help that you need. Silence doesn't help your progress. Talk about whatever inspires you.

266. Set expectations.

Share what you know about what is to come. Plan strategically. When others are informed, they can also make the best decisions. Others are not always able to read your mind.

267.   Buy some groceries.

It's time to nourish your body and soul. Get natural foods that are free of preservatives. Avoid takeout for a little bit. Make your own meal.

268.   Check the wires.

Make sure that your communication is clear. Prevent yourself from getting into a tangled mess. If you are already there, work to clear them away so that you can clear up any crossed signals.

269.   Evaluate the situation.

What lies before you may not be as you expect. Look at this from a different approach. Jumping to a conclusion will not help here. Look before you leap.

270.   Pull yourself up.

You are the only one who can bring yourself out of a rut. Find ways to build your strength. You have the power to change your frame of mind. Do something that makes you happy.

271. Just stop for a minute and listen.

You have decided your actions, but you are not taking time to listen to what you need. Take a time out. Are you listening to your body? Are you on the right course?

272. Deliver on your promises.

Complete your tasks. Do what you said you would do. Tie up the loose ends so you can move on to the next thing. Hold yourself accountable.

273.   Go to the zoo.

See the intrinsic behaviors of the animals around you. Understand how you are alike and how you are different. Learn about an animal that is different. You will be surprised at what you learn.

274.   Watch the clock.

Stick to your planned schedule. Distractions can deter you if you let them. You want to seize your opportunity and keep to your deadlines.

275. Walk barefoot.

Feel the sand through your toes. Enjoy the tickle of the grass on your feet. Step on the big rock. Connect to Mother Earth.

276. Give yourself a little lift.

Get your hair cut. Buy a new outfit or accessory. Do something that makes you feel good.

277.   Trust your elders.

Listen to the wisdom of those who are older than you. Look to stories of family history or pick up a relic of the past. Seek guidance from your ancestors.

278.   Release your crutch.

You do not need someone or something to hold you up. Stop leaning too much on others. You need to take your own steps. This doesn't mean that you won't fall. You will be stronger for getting yourself back up.

279.   Hear what nature must share.

Hear the cricket chirping. Note the sounds of the water. Listen to the whistle of the breeze. Acknowledge the silence.

280.   Seek the beauty in others.

When you look at someone always recognize that there is something beautiful in them. Find that beauty. We are all human. We are all beautiful.

281.　　Slow down.

The train you are on is going too fast. Make a point to look at the beauty all around you. Take in the aromas of your surroundings and breathe.

282.　　Recognize the divine within you.

You relate to all that is good in the world. If you are having trouble seeing that then connect with a friend who will help bring it out. Use your talents to help others.

283. Complete the cycle.

Everything has a beginning and an ending. You are nearing the end of a process or event in your life. Prepare for what is to come next.

284. Witness the opening of a flower.

See the beauty blossoming around you. Watch the change over a few days. Realize that you are flourishing.

285. Welcome your guide's wisdom.

Pay attention to that inner voice. Your direction is clear. Trust in yourself. Be still. Quiet your mind.

286. Be patient.

I'm sorry, but you need to wait a little longer. Make sure that you are ready for what you are about to receive. It will be worth the wait.

287.   Sing like the nightingale.

Use your voice to sing out loud. Connect to the emotion in a song. Feel the sense of release as you let it out. Explore your range.

288.   Take a walk.

Notice the light and shadows. Find the reflections around you. Appreciate the memory of your environment or the good parts of your neighborhood.

289.   Shoot for the stars.

Go after what you want. Even though your destination may seem out of reach you must keep striving for it. If you can see it, then you can attain it.

290.   Try again.

Sometimes things do not go as planned. And sometimes interruptions get in the way of reaching your target. This is not one and done. Don't give up.

291. Make the best use of your time.

Go for a massage or pedicure when your car is being worked on. Get laundry washed or dried when you are at the gym. Run the dishwasher before you go to bed. You will thank yourself for the efficiency.

292. Focus on your breath.

Take a few minutes to be calm. Sit in a chair. Breathe in. Breathe out. Breathe in. Breathe out. Breathe in. Breathe out. Be supported and at peace.

293. Organize one area of your home with love.

Look for spots of clutter and take some time to clean it up. Tackle that pile of mail in the corner. Get rid of those notes of things that have already been completed. Make the space work for you.

294. Go to the dentist.

Brush your teeth. Floss. Remove any plaque. Notice any sensitivity in your gums. Get any cavities filled. Make your next dental appointment.

295.   Let go of your ego.

Toss the ego out the window. Pinpoint what your work or creations can bring to others. The rewards are out there, you need to change the approach.

296.   Put your feet up.

It is time to rest your weary legs. Elevate them and lower your blood pressure. Bend and stretch. Feel the flow.

297.   Prepare for today.

Make a to-do list. Get resources ready.
Schedule meetings as necessary. Reach out
to others. Prepare to achieve.

298.   Let the sun and wind
kiss your cheek.

Spend time with nature. Use your senses
to experience what is around you. Be
grateful for your environment. Stand with
your arms open and receive nature's
energy.

299.   Trust in your faith.

Your beliefs form your reality. When you believe that everything will be ok, it will be. Stay positive.

300.   Exhibit openness and honesty.

Share your feelings. Do not hide what is bothering you. Harboring your feelings is only hurting you. Tell the truth.

301. Do something outside of your comfort zone.

Swim with the fish underwater. Climb the mountain. Try new foods. Give yourself the push and permission to try a new experience.

302. Step Away.

It is ok to remove yourself from difficult situations. You will come back refreshed and focused. Give yourself permission to escape for a little bit. You deserve some grace as do other people.

303.   Develop yourself.

You are rare and fabulous. You don't need to pretend to like something that you don't. You don't need to emulate another persona. Be true to who you are. Grow and expand on your abilities.

304.   Continue your studies.

There is always more to learn. Look for additional ways to grow. Further the studies that you have already been exploring. Find ways that your knowledge can help others.

305.   Invite a guest to your table.

Share a meal with a friend or family member. Enjoy cooking a meal for someone that you care about. Or be open to the opportunity to meet a new friend.

306.   Lay out your clothes for tomorrow.

Set yourself up for success. Take the steps needed to organize your thoughts and space. Outline the tasks to achieve your plan of action. Make your dreams a reality.

307.   Embrace the Struggle.

Apply your energy to overcome any issues. You are defined on how your rise from challenges, like the phoenix out of ashes. Strive to see the success that you know is yours.

308.   Beautify the world.

Create. Pick up trash. Plant flowers. Find a way to contribute to the beauty in this world.

309.   Let go of your problems.

It's time to dive right in and do what you can to overcome your issues. There could be a lot of talking to work through them. This time will be filled with emotion, but ultimately working through them will be worth the effort.

310.   Take control of your destiny.

When the direction is not clear forge your own way. You do not need to follow another's footprints. Chart your own course. You've got this!

311.   Free yourself from stuff.

Keep what is truly meaningful to you. Take a photo of the things you want to remember but no longer need. If you had to pack a suitcase of what was important, would the thing in your hand be selected?

312.   Let your heart be open to new situations.

When you automatically go to no you are shut off. Don't shrug at an offer that might not seem appealing at first. Do some research to see how it might play out. You might enjoy yourself.

313. Feel love in your heart.

You are loved in this world and beyond. Feel it in your heart. Put your hands on opposite shoulders and squeeze. This is my hug for you.

314. Take a day off.

It is time to relax. And relaxing does not mean checking things off a personal to-do list. It means playing a game, going to a spa, talking with family and friends, or watching movies. You need to recuperate.

315.   Broaden your horizons.

As you climb the mountain, stop along the way to look around. As you take a walk along the trail look up at the colors of the sky. There is so much beauty in this world. Make the effort to see it and enjoy the view.

316.   Paint the house.

It's time to do the painting that you have been putting off. Prep your walls. Get out the power washer for your deck. Break out the brushes and get to it. Refresh your environment.

317.   Get some legal advice.

Plan your will. Check your beneficiaries. Review your estate, no matter what size it is. Monitor your trademark. Make sure that you understand your rights and obligations.

318.   Move if the opportunity comes.

Opportunities rarely present themselves twice. If you really want it, then you'll have to move fast. You may not get a second chance. Hesitation or indecision may allow an opportunity to pass.

319. Set the stage.

Design your life how you want it to be.
Reorganize a room. Put in motion the steps
to change your story. Establish the
environment for your first scene.

320. Remove the weeds.

A pollinator garden can become overrun
with weeds. Take care of it to keep the
butterflies and bees thriving. We need
them for our survival. Do your part to
cleanup. The earth is our only true home.

321. Align with your desired state of mind.

Get mentally prepared for what you know is to come. Be present. Let your emotions guide you where you want to be. Remember you control them.

322. Ask for what you want.

If no one knows what you want how can they help you get it. You need to start asking. Ask the universe. Ask a friend or family member. Pray. Release your desires so they can be heard.

323. Take some time to sleep.

Listen to your body when it tells you that it needs to sleep. You need to rejuvenate the body and soul. Take a nap or go to bed early tonight.

324. Monitor your health.

Track your food intake. Tune into your body as it changes with how your move and what you eat. Pay attention and recognize what makes you feel the best.

325.   Move your body.

Get up off the couch, chair, bed, etc. You need to move. Seek out philosophies and change your mind. Consider a change of residence.

326.   Write a poem.

Observe what is going on around you. Get your feelings out on paper. Let nature or the city inspire you. Go outside and find creativity.

327.   Listen to uplifting music.

Put on some music that makes you smile and want to move. Let loose. Have a dance party!

328.   Complete a puzzle.

Exercise your brain. Challenge yourself to do something new. Looks for the clues that you need to put the pieces together. Try something hard that you have been putting off.

329.   Give yourself a treat.

You have been working hard and deserve a reward. Go out for some ice cream or a manicure. Plan your next vacation.

330.   Consider the consequences.

Think about what will happen once you say those words or take that action. Is it worth it? Contemplate the reaction before acting on it.

331.   Clear the Air.

Put on that dehumidifier. Open your feelings and set the record straight. It is not worthwhile to hold that grudge.

332.   Show your strength.

You have weathered the storm. It is not the time to think about what you should have done. Demonstrate your courage with the next thing you build.

333. Pull out the sticky notes.

Find a different method to organize your work. Be careful not to forget an important task. Review the open items and complete one. Every step gets you closer to the goal.

334. Manage yourself.

Compartmentalize the areas of your life to address what you want to achieve. Be realistic on what you can do in one day, week, month. Seek additional ways to pull off the work.

335.   Help a friend.

It can be hard for some people to ask for help. If you see a friend who needs assistance offer it. You'll both feel better in the end.

336.   Give yourself time to acclimate.

Change is going to come your way. Some you may choose others you may not. Allow yourself time for the adjustment and then find your way.

337.   Clear off your desk.

It's time to get rid of the paper. Reorganize to make the space work for you. Provide clear access to what you need readily available. Bring peace and clarity to your work environment.

338.   Open your eyes.

You may be missing something that is right in front of you. When you rush you can miss so much beauty. Look closely at what is going on around you. That lost item may not be so lost.

339. Focus on equality.

Everyone has a role in this world. The part you play may help someone understand a concept, give someone hope, or change the way we think or live. It's up to you to decide what you want that to be, but the more you acknowledge and appreciate others equally important role, the happier you will be.

340. Rally up your resources.

You are not defeated. Don't give up before it is over. Put in a good effort for what you want. There is still time to win. Keep going.

341.   Explore a new place.

Seek out an unfamiliar area. Check out a modern restaurant. Go to a museum that you have not been to yet. Look for a park and take a walk. Learn about something unique.

342.   Find the amazing things that are happening near you.

Look for the good in people. Watch kind actions unfold in front of you. Concentrate on the best thing that happened today. Acknowledge what is good in your life.

343.   Research a different culture.

Read a story from a different land or time in history. Think about what life may be like if you were in that place or time. Research the customs of that community. Find and prepare to attend a local event hosted by another culture.

344.   Stretch.

Reach your arms to the sky. Roll your head from side to side. Extend your legs. Flex your ankles. Wiggle each toe. Release your jaw. Relieve your stress.

345.   Increase your gratitude.

Stop wishing for greener pastures. Take stock in what you already have and recognize what led you to your current situation. Being grateful for what is positive among difficult situations can make that which is hard, easier. Find the positive in a difficult situation to make a difference in the long run.

346.   Be true to yourself.

Don't live your life the way that others think you should. Live the life that you want to live. Live your truth.

347.   Choose to hope for what you desire.

The power of hope is so strong. It can have a great impact on mindset, even if whatever is being hoped for doesn't come to fruition. The act of hoping for something is worthwhile. There is always something that deserves hope.

348.   Dress for the weather.

Check the weather. Wear layers to accommodate changing temperatures. Pack appropriately during changing seasons if you are going on a trip. Remember your umbrella.

349.   Eliminate what no longer suits you.

Focus on the things that you want to be in your life. Donate, recycle, or trash what you no longer need. You'll feel better having the space available. Be free from whatever is holding you back.

350.   Thread the needle.

Move very carefully through your current situation. Look at what is on both sides. You can make your way through with caution. It's not the time to be reckless.

351.   Define your purpose.

Everyone on this planet is here for a reason. From every ant to every eagle to every human. Yes, you have a purpose. And it does not need to be a grandiose thing to change the world. Sometimes you just need to be there to support your family or friends.

352.   Enjoy the journey.

Remember as you travel through life that it's not the end destination that carries the most reward. It is those who you encounter and the experiences that you have along the way that make it all worthwhile. Express thanks to those who have made a difference in that journey.

353. Respond with patience.

You may be feeling like you need immediate gratification, but it is in your best interest to wait. The waiting may be tough but stay focused on your goal. Look for different avenues if the first road didn't get you where you needed to be.

354. Fix the problem.

Why do you constantly deal with things that are broken? It's time to get out the glue and fix them. Look at the simple things that can improve your quality of life.

355.   Pivot.

Your plan to do something at a particular time may not go as you thought. Adjust and change direction. Go with the flow. You will still be able to get everything done, just not in the order that you planned. Move to the next thing that you can do.

356.   Believe in what you can accomplish.

Don't doubt your abilities. You have what it takes to succeed. Practice builds confidence.

357.   Join the caravan.

It is time to join the crowd. You have spent enough time solo. Go on a group trip and embrace the world. Get out and meet new people.

358.   Set your sights on what you want.

I believe in you. You have the power to complete your goals. Give it all that you've got. If you have not figured it out yet, dream big and write your goal list with serious, silly, short-term, and long-term goals. You can do it.

359.   Dance in the Rain.

Let go of your inhibitions. Be free from the fear that is holding you back. Do something a little out of character for you. Be free.

360.   Embrace the imperfection to move forward.

Over analysis causes projects to halt. Sometimes it is more important to keep going then to have everything perfect. Ask yourself, "Are my high expectations benefitting me and others?" Your perfectionism can hold you back.

361.   Go to the doctor.

Get your annual check-up scheduled. Seek insight into the problem that is currently bothering you. Look for a practitioner that treats the whole person, not just symptoms.

362.   Give something old new life.

Reuse things around you in creative way. Focus on sustainability. Look at the impact of the waste around you and find ways to recycle.

363.   Buy yourself a present.

It is ok to splurge on yourself occasionally. Go for something meaningful for you. Celebrate you! Your happiness is worth it.

364.   Support a small business.

Look for the things that you need in your local community. Appreciate the skills of your neighbors. Celebrate the abilities of those in your area. Invest in your community.

365.   Turn the page.

Look at the next chapter of your life with the awe and excitement that it deserves. Set some goals on what you want to achieve. Take charge of your own evolution and get to work.

Leap Year Bonus

366.   Make a four-year plan.

Consider all that you want to achieve before the next leap year. Remain flexible in working with what the world has to offer you. Listen to your intuition and follow it, even if it diverts from your plan. Reflect on this in another four years.

About the Author

Cynthia I. Wilson is a writer, photographer, librarian, life coach, and spiritual advisor. She has been published several poetry anthologies. Cynthia published her first children's book, "The Tooth Fairy Lost Her Way" in 2022. She resides in Delaware County, Pennsylvania with her husband, two children, and their cat, Garnett. Cynthia has a special knack for finding 4 leaf clovers and likes to share her luck with others.

For more information on Cynthia's writing and publications see:
https://cynthiawilson.net/writing/publications-exhibitions/

About the Book

"This Message Is For You!" provides bite size words of wisdom to encourage you to take action to improve your life. The micro motivators aim to give you that simple next step to answer the question, what should I do now? You will be able to take the simple nudges provided by the micro motivators and make the first step into manifesting the things that you want in your life. Are you ready to take the next step?

Want to go deeper with the messages?
Check out Cynthia's podcast.
A list of podcast platforms can be found at:
https://cynthiawilson.net/this-message-is-for-you/